T0349148

MID-CENTURY MODERN

ICONS OF DESIGN

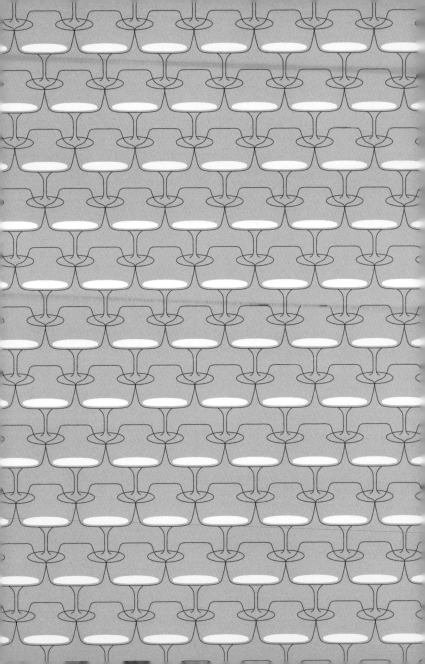

MID-CENTURY MODERN

ICONS OF DESIGN

Illustrations by Here Design

Texts by Frances Ambler

With 96 illustrations

First published in the United Kingdom in 2016
as *Mid-Century Modern: Icons of Design*
(set of 4 concertina books) by Thames & Hudson Ltd,
181A High Holborn, London WC1V 7QX

First published in the United States of America in 2016
as *Mid-Century Modern: Icons of Design*
(set of 4 concertina books) by Thames & Hudson Inc.,
500 Fifth Avenue, New York, New York 10110

This revised and updated format 2018
Reprinted 2024

Mid-Century Modern: Icons of Design
© 2016 and 2018 Thames & Hudson Ltd, London
Illustrations © 2016 and 2018 Inkipit
Texts by Frances Ambler

British Library Cataloguing-in-Publication Data
A catalogue record for this book is available from
the British Library

Library of Congress Control Number
2017963800

ISBN 978-0-500-02203-0

Printed in China by RR Donnelley

MIX
Paper | Supporting
responsible forestry
FSC® C144853
www.fsc.org

Be the first to know about our new releases,
exclusive content and author events by visiting
thamesandhudson.com
thamesandhudsonusa.com
thamesandhudson.com.au

CONTENTS

INTRODUCTION

Think mid-century design and what's the first thing that you picture? Perhaps it's the fibreglass curves of an Eames RAR chair? The distinctive silhouette of an Artichoke lamp? Or the playful form of a Ball clock? It's a testament to the power of mid-century design that not only do such objects come so readily to mind, but also that they're all still in production and every bit as desirable today. What's even more astounding is the range of mid-century designs that can justify being described as icons: the term also applies to the likes of scooters and speakers, typewriters and tea sets, all of which helped shape the look of the period.

If these designs look fresh to 21st-century eyes, just imagine their impact when they were first revealed. Although this book includes a handful of examples from the 1930s, the majority of designs date to the period following the Second World War, and are born out of its legacy. The war both pushed designers to find creative solutions — as with the Antelope chair, made using steel because of shortages of other materials — and acted as a technological catalyst — an innovative leg splint, for instance, suggested plywood's potential future uses to Charles and Ray Eames. Designers displaced by the war, such as the former teachers and students of the German Bauhaus, helped the international exchange of ideas.

While designers dealt, sometimes obsessively, with specific conundrums (Poul Henningsen notably created over one hundred lamps during his lifetime to master the effect of candlelight with electric lighting), they were united by their concern for a much larger question: what should modern life look like? In response, classics were taken apart and remade, from Gino Sarfatti's stripped-back chandelier to the Eameses' Model 670, a contemporary version of the English club chair. Such designs embraced a new way of living that extended to work and leisure, as well as the home. They were invented for a society that was to be less formal and less hierarchical — largely informed by the sentiment, voiced by Russel Wright, that 'good design is for everyone'.

The resulting designs, however, are far from uniform in their approach. Although some were intended to be mass-produced, others are handmade works of art. Some celebrate the machine age, others look to natural forms for inspiration. Such diversity created an astonishing array of designs and it's a testament to the creativity of the period that — whether chair, table, lighting or object — it produced many more examples of iconic design than it is possible to include here. While each of the selected icons has its own remarkable story, it's when they are considered together that the mid-century legacy is most apparent. It's a collection of unique voices united in their determination to create a better world — creating an influential and inspiring body of ideas and designs from which we still benefit today.

THE ICONS

MODEL 42

BIRCH AND BEECH

ALVAR AALTO
ARTEK, c. 1932

Although an architect by training, Aalto considered every
detail of modern living – from lighting to bath rails – worthy
of attention. Like many other Scandinavian designers, he
was a 'soft modernist', favouring craftsmanship and organic
materials over machine-made. While Marcel Breuer created
chairs from tubular steel, Aalto thought such designs were
'unsatisfactory from a human point of view', and he looked to
create similarly modern forms using birch and beech instead.

Aalto's work would be cited as an influence on an array
of designers in the post-war period, from Ray and Charles
Eames to Carlo Mollino and Aalto's compatriot Eero Saarinen.
Many of his designs, including the Model 42 chair, are still
in production today through Artek, the company he founded
with his wife, the architect and glass designer Aino Aalto.

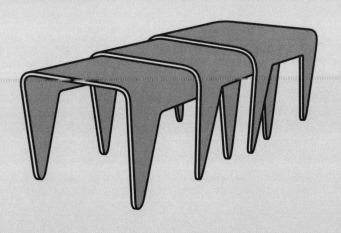

NESTING TABLES

BEECH PLYWOOD

MARCEL BREUER
VENESTA FOR ISOKON, 1936

———

Between leaving Germany and arriving in the States, several members of the Bauhaus lived in London's Lawn Road Flats. Jack Pritchard, the entrepreneur behind the stylishly modern Isokon building (as the Flats were also known), used the opportunity to commission the likes of Walter Gropius and Marcel Breuer to design for his Isokon Furniture Company.

Breuer was then known for his use of tubular steel – particularly in the 1920s Wassily chair – but Pritchard felt plywood was more suited to the English sensibility. Breuer's experiments with the material produced five pieces for Isokon, including his famous Long Chair of 1936.

The loss of their plywood supply during the War caused Isokon to close, not to be revived until the 1960s. Meanwhile, inspired by the work of Breuer, and also Alvar Aalto, designers such as Charles and Ray Eames and Eero Saarinen had re-imagined plywood's potential themselves.

PERNILLA CHAISE

LAMINATE STEAM-BENT BEECH AND CANVAS

BRUNO MATHSSON
KARL MATHSSON, 1936

After apprenticing in his father's cabinetmaking firm, Bruno
Mathsson began experimenting with the possibilities of bent
wood and his furniture of the 1930s is seen as a forerunner of
the softer Scandinavian style of modernism. Mathsson's bent
birch or beech frames were as economic as a design by Le
Corbusier, but suggested an organic alternative to tubular
steel. Woven strips of leather or canvas took the place of
traditional upholstery.

In the 1950s, however, while other designers devoted their
attention to catering for new ways of living by using new
materials, Mathsson instead focused on architecture, only
returning to furniture design in the 1960s after he took over
the family business. His later collaborations included the 1964
Super-Elliptical table with mathematician and inventor
Piet Hein, another design elegant in its economy.

AMERICAN MODERN TABLEWARE

CERAMIC

RUSSEL WRIGHT
STEUBENVILLE, 1937

———

In 1950, Russel Wright and his wife Mary Small Einstein released their book, *Guide to Easier Living*. It encapsulated their design philosophy that life should be easier and more relaxed, and designs for living should be functional, affordable and hardwearing. These were the principles guiding Wright's American Modern tableware, a range so popular it had sold over 250 million pieces by the end of the 1950s.

Unlike other pieces of tableware, these used smooth, organic forms that would not, according to Wright 'attract more attention than the food'. Originally available in six colours – 'seafoam' blue, coral, chartreuse, grey, white and 'bean' brown – unlike other tableware sets, it could be mixed and matched. Being made from earthenware also meant that the collection was affordable for the average American. As consumers embraced the range during the 1940s and '50s, it demonstrated that Wright's proclamation that 'good design is for everyone' could indeed be true.

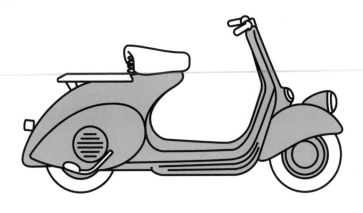

VESPA

CORRADINO D'ASCANIO
PIAGGIO, 1940S

––––

What better symbol of the *Dolce Vita* than the Vespa?
It rode its way into public affections in the 1940s – selling
over a million in its first ten years – and has remained there ever
since: coveted, collected and customized.

One part of its undeniable appeal is, of course, its good looks.
The streamlined shell – which protected the wheels, engine and
petrol tank, as well as shielding its rider from the dirt of the road
– brought a new look to the streets.

Moreover, the Vespa symbolized a desire for personal freedom,
offering an affordable way to escape from the challenges
of daily life. No wonder it enticed the young Modernists of
Britain, and countless others since. Who hasn't fantasized
about escaping into the sunset, perhaps – in the style of 1953's
Roman Holiday – with Audrey Hepburn in tow?

MODEL IN-20 DINING TABLE

LACQUERED BIRCH AND STEEL

ISAMU NOGUCHI
HERMAN MILLER, 1944

———

Born in Los Angeles to a Japanese father and American mother, Noguchi spent much of his life travelling between the two countries. Interned himself, he campaigned for the rights of Japanese–American citizens in the United States during the Second World War. However, it was towards the end of the War that he began to be noticed for both his sculpture and his furniture designs. His relationship with Herman Miller was set in motion when one of his designs was used to illustrate a George Nelson article entitled 'How To Build a Table'.

Noguchi believed that 'everything is sculpture'. This table, with its wooden 'rudder' leg balanced with two metal hairpin legs, is a persuasive argument in favour of his statement.

DCW CHAIR

BIRCH PLYWOOD

CHARLES AND RAY EAMES
HERMAN MILLER, 1945

This 1940s classic – still in production – inspired countless other designs, as well as establishing the reputation of Charles and Ray Eames. The couple met at Cranbrook Art Academy, renowned for being one of the United States' most progressive design schools, and married in 1941. The success of their design for a moulded plywood leg splint not only enabled them to open their own office, but also demonstrated how the material could be adapted to the contours of the human body.

In their 'Plywood group', the Eameses applied this idea to furniture. Ingenious designs including the Lounge Chair Wood (LCW) and this Dining Chair Wood (DCW) showed how modern forms and production techniques could still be used to create an organic feel. Perhaps more significantly, they brought the Eameses to the attention of Herman Miller, the company that would go on to introduce their work to a much wider market.

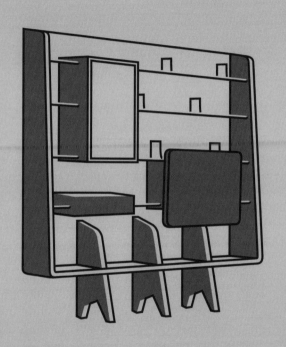

BOOKCASE

WALNUT, MAPLE, GLASS AND BRASS

GIO PONTI
COLOMBO, 1945

———

Although Gio Ponti had already established his reputation prior to the Second World War, he embraced the post-war necessity of rebuilding Italy, grasping the key role that its designers could play in that task. Ponti was known for new ideas, forging connections and his boundless energy.

Ponti conjured up designs that were rooted in his country's history but he could also turn his talents to more modern pieces, as shown in the playful treatment of this bookcase, which seems to perch almost magically on top of its three legs. Ponti also successfully collaborated with Piero Fornasetti, the shapes of his furniture perfectly suiting the artist's fanciful forms. These pieces continue to achieve huge sums at auction.

CA 832 ARMCHAIR

WALNUT AND UPHOLSTERY

FRANCO ALBINI
CASSINA, 1946

The architect and designer Franco Albini worked with Gio
Ponti before establishing his own practice in Milan in 1930.
He is frequently cited as an important member of the Italian
Neo-Rationalist movement, designing furniture that made
no attempt to conceal the raw materials or the underlying
production process. Albini's Gala chairs of 1950, for example,
were made using inexpensive, easily available wicker, while
the walnut frame of the Ca 832 is an essential element of
the chair's elegant aesthetic.

Albini's relationship with Cassina – a company known for
nurturing Italian design talent – began with chairs, but also
encompassed designs such as a 'Sailboat' bookshelf, which
was so forward-thinking that it was only put into production
in the 21st century.

MODEL 4658 HOME OFFICE DESK

WALNUT, STEEL AND LEATHER

GEORGE NELSON
HERMAN MILLER, 1946

––––

George Nelson studied architecture at Yale but initially became known within the design world for his championing of European practitioners through his writing for publications such as *Pencil Points* and *Architecture* magazine. Building a reputation for both his ideas and connections, Nelson was invited to become Director of Design at Herman Miller in 1945, and this desk dates from the subsequent year.

Combining walnut, steel and leather, the desk demonstrates how Nelson felt even the most traditional of forms could be made modern. While he created chairs such as the Coconut that were made for relaxation, he also saw that work environments could be transformed. In the 1960s Nelson worked on Herman Miller's 'Action Office', which attempted to reinvent the furniture of the modern workplace. One consequence of the project would be the development of the office cubicle.

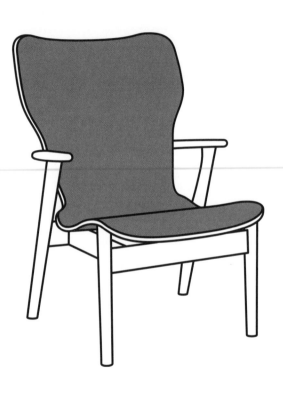

DOMUS LOUNGE CHAIR

BIRCH

ILMARI TAPIOVAARA
KERAVAN PUUTEOLLISUUS, 1946

————

Ilmari Tapiovaara's designs were shaped by the austerity of post-war Finland. His work was in some ways a continuation of that of Alvar Aalto – whom he admired greatly – creating simple forms from natural materials. Tapiovaara believed that good design was for everyone, and many of his furniture designs were for public spaces. His most famous design was the Domus chair, named after the academy for which it was made and also available as a lounge chair with a taller back. This chair was designed to be comfortable for students but affordable to produce. Being stackable, it also saved space.

Initially manufactured by Keravan Puuteollisuus – where Tapiovaara became commercial and artistic director in 1941 – the chair is now available through Artek. Knoll sold millions of the Domus chair in the United States under the name 'Model 140'. Lightweight and stacked easily into crates, the Domus was perhaps the perfect chair to import.

MODEL 4765 MAGAZINE TREE

WALNUT AND BIRCH

EDWARD WORMLEY
DUNBAR, 1947

———

In 1931, aged only 23, Edward Wormley became Director of Design at Dunbar, hired to rejuvenate sales at this Indiana furniture company. The working relationship would last just under forty years, during which time Dunbar became one of the leading producers of modern furniture in the United States.

Initially unsure in what direction to take his brief, Wormley had experimented both with more traditional and more contemporary forms. It quickly became obvious that the latter designs were selling more strongly. While continuing to offer updated versions of more traditional styles, Wormley also created designs that were undeniably original and desirable in their own right, as demonstrated by the striking graphic outline of this magazine tree.

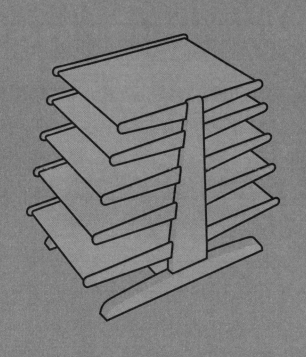

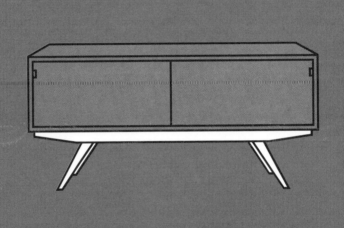

MODEL 122 CABINET

BIRCH, LACQUERED WOOD, PANDANUS AND LEATHER

FLORENCE KNOLL
KNOLL, 1947

———

Hans Knoll founded his company in 1938, inspired by the realization that modern buildings would require well-designed, equally modern furniture. Florence Schust – who had worked and studied with various members of the Bauhaus group – was hired as a designer, and the couple married in 1946.

Florence guided the aesthetics of Knoll, as well as designing many pieces herself. In designs such as the Model 122 cabinet, pared-back modernist shapes were created in harmonious combinations of different materials. The cabinet was practical too, with its two sliding doors concealing a drawer and seven adjustable shelves. Florence considered furniture one element in what she described as 'total design', the balance of different elements in an intelligently planned space.

After Hans' death in 1955, Florence took over at Knoll. Through the designs she commissioned, as well as her own, she continued to shape the look of modern American interiors.

MODEL 4755 BALL WALL CLOCK

ENAMELLED ALUMINIUM, BRASS, ENAMELLED STEEL AND LACQUERED WOOD

GEORGE NELSON
HOWARD MILLER CLOCK COMPANY, 1948

——

George Nelson's much-imitated Ball clock proved that clocks did not just have to be functional – they also could be fun. Through his writing and editing, as well as his work for Herman Miller, Nelson established relationships with other design innovators and it's said this clock came about thanks to a session with Buckminster Fuller and Isamu Noguchi, along with Irving Harper, a designer in Nelson's studio.

Released five years before Charles and Ray Eames employed the charm of colourful wooden balls for their Hang it all coat rack, this design demonstrated that clocks could be modern and covetable objects in their own right. Originally available in six different colour combinations, the Ball clock – like that coat rack – has been released in many more colours over the subsequent years, including a 'natural' version.

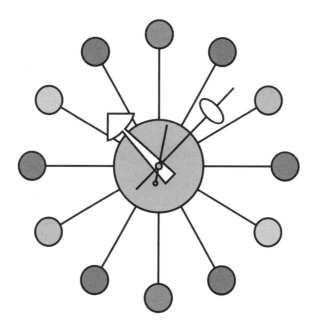

MODEL 654L SIDE CHAIR

BIRCH AND WEBBED CANVAS SEATING

JENS RISOM
KNOLL, c. 1949

––––

Of the twenty-five items pictured in Knoll's first catalogue,
released in 1941, Jens Risom was responsible for fifteen.
Risom's 600 series of tables and chairs were created directly
in response to the shortages brought about by the war. What
would have been off-cast pieces of wood were transformed
into frames, while discarded military materials were woven
into supportive lattices. Risom described the designs as
'very basic, very simple, inexpensive, easy to make'. Despite
their apparent simplicity, he managed to make these basic
components look completely modern.

Risom's relationship with Knoll was cut short by the war and,
later in the 1940s, he would form his own design studio. His love
of using materials in fresh, unexpected ways, however, remained
a constant throughout his career.

MAGAZINE TABLE

WALNUT

JENS RISOM
JENS RISOM DESIGN, c. 1949

––––

Jens Risom's work for Knoll in the early 1940s had gained him considerable attention. However, post-war, as Florence Knoll pursued Bauhaus-inspired ideals, Risom decided to establish his own studio to enjoy more freedom and explore his own interests.

Risom's designs combined the traditions of his Danish heritage with the modern thrust of American design. He created beautiful furniture for contemporary lives. This formula was immensely successful and Jens Risom Design grew to be the third largest furniture company in the United States. This table appeared in the first comprehensive Jens Risom Design catalogue, alongside the slogan 'furniture with a signature'.

Despite Risom's fame, it's only recently that his most famous designs have been put back into production. The British companies Rocket and Benchmark have reissued eleven pieces by Risom, including this table.

MODEL JH 501 ROUND CHAIR

OAK AND CANE

HANS WEGNER
JOHANNES HANSEN, 1949

——

From over 500 chairs designed by Hans Wegner in his lifetime, it was the Round chair that became simply known as 'the chair'. It had been dubbed 'the world's most beautiful chair' by an American interiors magazine in 1950, but it was its starring role in the 1961 televised US presidential debates between Nixon and Kennedy that really took Danish design into the American living room.

Like all of Wegner's designs, this chair emphasized purity of form, illustrating his wish to 'cut down to the simplest possible elements of four legs, a set and combined top rail and arm rest'. However, with its craftsmanship, and gentle, inviting curves, it represented a softer modernism, in contrast to the more austere, pre-war designs.

MODEL 1114 COFFEE TABLE

MAPLE, SECURIT GLASS AND BRASS

CARLO MOLLINO
APELLI & VARESIO, *c.* 1950

'Everything is possible as long as it is fantastic,' said the Italian designer Carlo Mollino, famed for both his larger-than-life persona and the sense of fancy that he brought to modern design. His influences ranged from the Surrealists to Alvar Aalto and his furniture was unashamedly organic. Sometimes zoomorphic forms were suggested, other times made literal by timber shaped as horns, hoofs and, in the case of the Model 1114 coffee table, antlers.

Only ever made in limited numbers, and often specifically created for particular buildings, Mollino's designs remain highly sought-after. In 2005, another glass-topped table – the 'Reale' – sold for $3,824,000.

TABLE LAMP

RICE PAPER AND ENAMELLED WIRE

ISAMU NOGUCHI
OZEKI AND CO., 1950S

———

Isamu Noguchi would describe himself first and foremost as
a sculptor. In the 1920s, he had been an assistant to Constantin
Brancusi in Paris. However, Noguchi brought his artist's eye to
his designs, particularly to the much-imitated paper lanterns he
designed over several decades with Ozeki and Co.

While visiting Gifu, a Japanese town known for its traditional
paper products, Noguchi was invited to design a new lantern,
in the hope that it would create a desirable export product.
This commission would eventually become more than 100
lamps, each one based on traditional Japanese paper but
combined with metal supports and adapted for electric bulbs.
There were ceiling lamps, floor lamps and – as in this design
– table lamps, all demonstrating the global influences on
mid-century modernism in its most sculptural, but also most
accessible form.

RAR ROCKING CHAIR

MOULDED FIBREGLASS WITH STEEL AND BIRCH LEGS/ROCKERS

CHARLES AND RAY EAMES
HERMAN MILLER, 1950

———

Following their experiments with plywood – which had produced the likes of the DCW chair – and their 1948 'Low Cost Furniture' designs for a competition held at New York's Museum of Modern Art, Charles and Ray Eames moved on to exploring another material: fibreglass. It was developed by the military in the Second World War but the Eameses sensed its potential for making low-cost furniture and used it to realize their aim of bringing 'the most of the best to the greatest number of people for the least'.

A moulded fibreglass shell forms the basis of a series of chairs, combined with various bases to create different looks economically. Compare their 'Dining Armchair Rod' (DAR), for example, with the 'Rocking Armchair Rod', where birch rockers give the traditional rocking chair a radical makeover.

COFFEE TABLE

WALNUT, IRON AND COPPER

JENS RISOM
JENS RISOM DESIGN, *c.* 1950

———

Educated in Europe but establishing his name in the United States, Jens Risom combined both design traditions to create modern pieces of furniture. As might be expected from his Danish background, Risom described wood as his favourite material. However, in contrast to the lighter woods favoured by the likes of Hans Wegner, Risom preferred the darker walnut. 'It has a richness and a grain characteristic that lends itself to all kinds of things,' he explained. Walnut particularly suited being used in combination with warmer metals, as seen on this coffee table. Such compositions of different materials would be a hallmark of his designs.

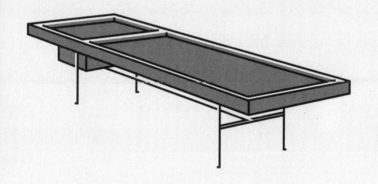

LEGGERA CHAIR

WALNUT AND CANE

GIO PONTI
CASSINA, 1950

———

Already an established name before the Second World War, Gio Ponti embraced post-war opportunities with characteristic gusto, designing for 120 different companies and creating everything from ceramics to coffee machines. The Leggera chair and the subsequent Superleggera – which was to become one of his most famous designs – were both designed for Cassina.

They were born out of the desire to make a modern, lightweight chair ('Leggera' means 'light' in Italian). Although the designs were elegant and contemporary, they nodded to Italy's artisanal traditions, their cane seats being inspired by the woven straw seat of the 19th-century Chiavara chair. The Superleggera weighed only 1.7kg and, to underline the point, its 1957 advert depicted a child lifting it with ease.

COFFEE TABLE

WALNUT, WALNUT BURL AND BRASS

ICO AND LUISA PARISI
SINGER & SONS, *c.* 1950

———

Ico Parisi was an architect, filmmaker and designer who turned his hand to everything from lighting to ceramics; his wife Luisa was a former student of Gio Ponti. They founded their design studio in 1948 and, while they did work independently, they sometimes also collaborated on designs such as this coffee table.

Designed for the American furniture manufacturer Singer & Sons, it demonstrates a resemblance to Ponti's designs, especially with its skeletal legs enhanced with brass detailing. Singer & Sons were known for exploring the appetite for Italian design in the United States and by 1954 its owner Josef Singer had commissioned designs from the likes of Ponti and Carlo Mollino, as well as Ico and Luisa Parisi.

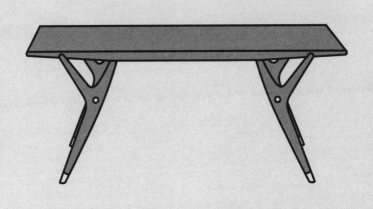

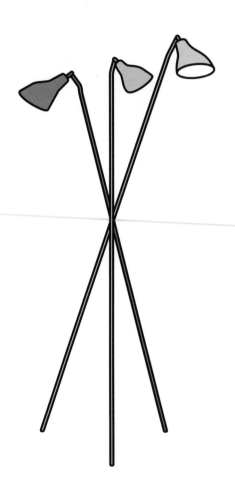

TRIPOD FLOOR LAMP

ENAMELLED METAL AND BRASS

GINO SARFATTI
ARREDOLUCE, c. 1950

––––

Unlike many designers of the mid-century period for whom lighting was just one element of their output, Gino Sarfatti focused on it alone, becoming a master in his field and helping elevate the status of the Italian lighting industry as a whole. His interest was sparked while working in a lampshade-manufacturing factory and, over the next thirty plus years, he would go on to design hundreds of lamps.

While Sarfatti's later designs became more functional, there's a sense of light-heartedness running through his work of the early 1950s. The cheerful colours used in this floor lamp chime with a sense of post-war optimism and also suggest that lights were every bit as deserving of a place in the modern interior as an innovative piece of seating or a brand new set of streamlined tableware.

ANTELOPE CHAIR

BENT STEEL RODS AND PLY SEAT

ERNEST RACE
ERNEST RACE LTD, 1951

———

If some mid-century designs were inspired by technological advancements that had been accelerated by the Second World War, others were innovative solutions to the shortage of materials it created. The Antelope was an example of the latter, enabled by Ernest Race's partnership with the engineer J.W. Noel Jordan. Steel was rarely used for furniture at the time and the fabricating method used to shape the frame had never been employed in this context before.

As it was this design looked light and, thanks especially to its coloured wooden seat, optimistic, perfectly at home on the terraces and cafes of the 1951 Festival of Britain. It would be many people's first glimpse of this new, 'contemporary' style – a visual encapsulation of the Festival's promise there would be better things to come.

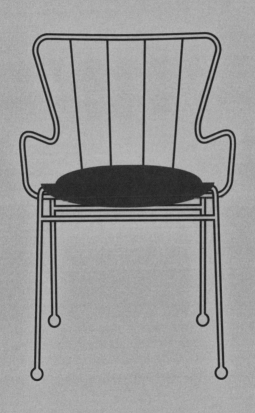

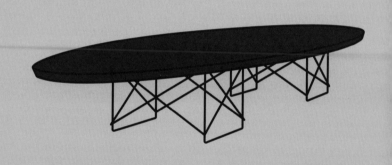

ETR TABLE

LAMINATE-OVER-PLYWOOD TABLETOP
AND ENAMELLED STEEL LEGS

CHARLES AND RAY EAMES
HERMAN MILLER, 1951

―――

Although the design is often referred to as the 'Surfboard' table – for obvious reasons – 'ETR' actually stands for Elliptical Table Rod, indicating this table's connection to the RAR rocking chair, and pointing to another innovation introduced by Charles and Ray Eames: the metal rods that supported both structures.

The impetus had apparently been born of Charles noticing all 'the fantastic things made of wire' and, after experimentation, the couple developed a mass production technique to simultaneously weld multiple wire rods. The resultant, deceptively sturdy metal structures became a hallmark of their design. They can be seen in the architectural base of the DSR chair (earning it the nickname of the 'Eiffel' chair), as well as the low twin supports for the long laminated plywood top of this coffee table.

SAWBUCK CHAIR

SOLID WOOD WITH VENEERED PLYWOOD BACK

HANS WEGNER
CARL HANSEN, 1951

'A chair is to have no backside,' said Hans Wegner. 'It should be beautiful from all sides and angles.' That's certainly true of the Sawbuck chair, as visually appealing as it is comfortable, with its sculptural frame and masterful handling of different woods exemplifying why Wegner is one of the most revered mid-century designers.

Trained as a cabinetmaker, despite many offers of work in the United States, Wegner preferred to stay in his own studio in Aarhus and remain immersed in the Danish design tradition. Although he worked with many manufacturers over his long career, the Sawbuck is one of the chairs he designed for Carl Hansen, a company that shared Wegner's interest in maintaining high-quality craftsmanship.

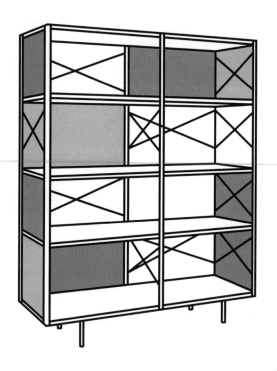

ESU 400

BIRCH PLYWOOD, ENAMELLED MASONITE, FIBREGLASS AND CHROME-PLATED STEEL

CHARLES AND RAY EAMES
HERMAN MILLER, 1952

The Eames Storage Unit (ESU) was intended to be flexible
– freestanding, multifunctional and adaptable. Its modular
elements made it easy to vary the arrangement of drawers and
panels, as well as the materials and finishes, according to its
owner's needs and taste.

Several aspects of the Eameses' work are reflected in the ESU.
It uses plywood and fibreglass, both materials experimented
with by the Eameses. More significantly, it links into the
Eameses' own home, which became their showcase for a
modern way of living. Their home was designed as part of
The Case Study Program, which asked architects to create
new, relatively affordable contemporary houses, using the
latest construction techniques. The Eameses' 'Case Study #8'
home, planned over the same period as their storage units, was
constructed using a steel frame, with different coloured panels
set into it – much like this cabinet, in fact.

TEEMA MINI SERVING SET

CERAMIC

KAJ FRANCK
IITTALA, 1952

We are now so accustomed to simple, functional servingware that it can be difficult to imagine how revolutionary Kaj Franck's Teema design was in the early 1950s. Originally released as the Kilta range, it was devised as an alternative to the period French and English-inspired sets that were a common feature on dining tables across Europe at the time.

Franck's range used very simple geometric shapes in a limited palette of colours. Colour was, he said, 'the only decoration needed'. The range could be stacked, mixed and matched and was made to last. More importantly, it was intended to be accessible to all and was priced as such. The design became a bestseller, with over 25 million of the combined lines sold and, by changing the way we serve food, has also changed the way we eat.

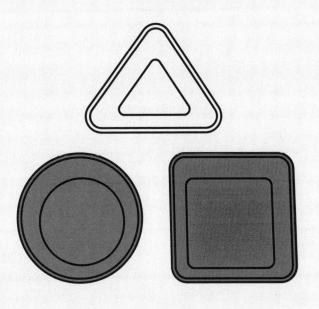

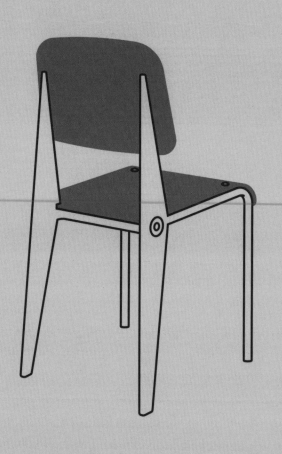

MODEL 300 CAFÉTERIA CHAIR

ENAMELLED STEEL AND ASH

JEAN PROUVÉ
ATELIERS JEAN PROUVÉ, c. 1952

———

Jean Prouvé is now described as being one of the greatest
French designers of the 20th century, with his original furniture
selling for sums that match his reputation. But Prouvé always
wanted his designs to be attainable and they were rooted in the
practical education he had in his apprenticeship as a blacksmith.
As he said, 'Never design anything that cannot be made.'

Prouvé's Standard chair of 1934, and this later variant, used
tubular steel for the front legs but thicker, hollow legs at the
back, as they would be subject to the most stress. He constantly
innovated, testing and refining mass production techniques
for metal in order to produce modern, functional furniture
suitable for schools and offices as well as homes. Perhaps most
importantly, Prouvé's chairs aren't only admired for their looks
or for their utility – they are also praised for their comfort.

PRIDE EIGHT-PIECE SET

STAINLESS STEEL

DAVID MELLOR
WALKER & HALL, 1953

––––

David Mellor combined the steel-making tradition of his hometown of Sheffield with a clean, curving and, most importantly, contemporary aesthetic. Pride was designed while Mellor was still a student at London's Royal College of Art, and not only helped launch his career but was also one of the post-war British products that could compete in an increasingly globalized marketplace. Mellor's other cutlery designs included the 'Embassy' designs, for use in British embassies, and 'Thrift', intended for public institutions, both dating to the 1960s.

However, beyond his position as 'cutlery king', Mellor also produced designs for objects as diverse as post boxes and traffic lights, earning him the honour – according to Sir Terence Conran – of being 'Britain's greatest post-war product designer'.

APPLIQUE À MURALE CINQ BRAS FIXES

ENAMELLED ALUMINIUM AND BRASS

SERGE MOUILLE
ATELIERS SERGE MOUILLE, 1953

___

While Italian lighting designers were pushing innovation through mass production, Serge Mouille's designs deliberately embraced the other extreme. They were hand-made pieces that he described as art.

Although primarily a sculptor, from 1953 to 1961 Mouille experimented with lighting. His uniformly black shell-like aluminium shades projected on spindly arms were undeniably sculptural and elegant in their purity. They were also slightly insectoid, appearing to crawl across floors and walls, especially when used in the form of a 'spider' wall-mounted lamp such as this one. But they were functional too: each individual head could be adjusted to create the lighting effect desired. Given the limited numbers produced, Mouille's lights were hugely influential and they remain highly desirable to this day.

MODEL 5313 MAGAZINE TABLE

LACQUERED WOOD

EDWARD WORMLEY
DUNBAR, 1953

Edward Wormley's name may be less well known today but in 1961 he appeared alongside the likes of Charles Eames, Eero Saarinen and Harry Bertoia in a *Playboy* feature celebrating 'Designs for Living'. In the article, Wormley revealed what Modernism meant to him. It was the 'freedom to mix, to choose, to change, to embrace the new but to hold fast to what is good'.

This goes some way to explain Wormley's varied portfolio, which demonstrates a mix of styles and inspirations and includes carpets, lamps and fabrics, as well as the furniture for Dunbar that made his name. His output was also vast – he created around 150 designs each year for Dunbar alone – helping to make his work an original but more affordable option for today's mid-century seeker.

MODEL 2072 LOLLIPOP
CHANDELIER

PLASTIC, ENAMELLED ALUMINIUM AND BRASS

GINO SARFATTI
ARTELUCE, 1953

———

Displaying the sense of playfulness that typified Gino
Sarfatti's lighting designs of the early 1950s, it's immediately
obvious why Model 2072 is more commonly referred to as the
Lollipop, or sometimes the Yo Yo, chandelier. Yet, despite the
childish nicknames, this chandelier takes the abstract forms of
something like an Alexander Calder sculpture and transforms
them into an everyday object for the home.

With his company Arteluce, Sarfatti produced hundreds of
lights of different types, but it is his reinterpretation of the
chandelier – a product perhaps not usually associated with
the pared-back forms of the mid-century period – that would
bring him the most acclaim.

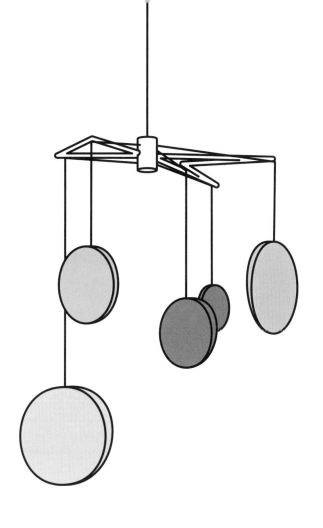

2000 TABLEWARE SERVICE

CERAMIC

RAYMOND LOEWY AND RICHARD LATHAM
ROSENTHAL, 1954

––––

The designs of Raymond Loewy, encompassing everything
from cars and cigarette packets to the Coca-Cola bottle,
had a huge influence on the look of modern America. He
created products for more than 200 companies including,
in the example of this tableware service designed with
Richard Latham, the German brand Rosenthal.

Rosenthal hired Loewy to update their image, as part of their
bid to break into the American market. His design is up-to-
the-minute, almost as futuristic as the name suggests. Its form
echoes the silhouettes of 1950s fashion – particularly the coffee
pot, which recalls the small-waisted, full-skirted designs of the
period – and encompasses the smooth, streamlined appearance
associated with Loewy's varied designs. The result more than
surpassed Rosenthal's brief. In fact, the service proved to be
so successful it remained in production until 1978.

ARMCHAIR

WALNUT AND UPHOLSTERY

GIO PONTI
REGUITTI, 1954

____

'Love it for its fantastic, adventurous and solemn creations' was how Gio Ponti extolled his profession of architecture. This passion for the varied possibilities of design was carried through every aspect of Ponti's work – from buildings to magazines, ceramics to paintings. It's hard to think of an aspect of Italian post-war design not touched by Ponti, especially given the impact of his influential *Domus* magazine, through which he shared his enthusiasms.

This resulted in a fascinating output of work that sometimes offered reinterpretations of familiar pieces and sometimes created more fantastical, zoomorphic pieces, but always displayed high-quality craftsmanship. The legs of this armchair, for example, look as if they might scuttle off at any moment, but they are balanced by the reassuring luxury of a richly upholstered cushion seat.

PORSCHE 356 SPEEDSTER

FERDINAND 'FERRY' PORSCHE
PORSCHE AG, 1954

The 356 came from 'Ferry' Porsche's desire to create a lightweight, smaller car that was built for speed. The initial models used the same engine as the Beetle, which Ferry's father and founder of the company Ferdinand Porsche had designed for Volkswagen. Changing the engine would be only one of many refinements made over its history.

Production of the 356 was initially slow and Porsche only made 52 in its first two years, but the American market provided the real impetus for change, with its demand for a sportier model that could challenge the dominance of British sports cars. To keep costs down, the Speedster model was stripped of trimmings, such as its wind-up windows, a change that actually helped enhance the car's streamlined look. The refined model was an immediate American hit, particularly in the sunnier states, with sales reaching a peak in 1957.

BUTTERFLY STOOL

ROSEWOOD AND BRASS

SORI YANAGI
TENDO, 1954

———

The Butterfly stool took the moulded plywood techniques
pioneered by Charles and Ray Eames and adapted them
to a Japanese aesthetic. The result is a graceful, apparently
timeless piece of design that has been compared to everything
from the gateway of a Shinto shrine to a Samurai helmet, as well
as to the butterfly wings that inspired the stool's name.

Sori Yanagi studied painting and architecture, and worked in
Charlotte Perriand's Tokyo office in the early 1940s prior to
founding his own studio in 1952. He is known for successfully
incorporating Japanese craftsmanship and traditions into his
designs for everyday life, whether that was a kettle or a piece
of cutlery.

POPSICLE DINING TABLE

LAMINATE AND LACQUERED WOOD

HANS BELLMANN
KNOLL, c. 1955

———

Swiss designer Hans Bellmann worked with Ludwig Mies van der Rohe prior to founding his own studio in Zurich in 1946. Typified by simple, uncluttered designs, Bellmann's work was a continuation of the Bauhaus legacy.

Although Bellmann designed furniture for a number of different manufacturers, pared-back but striking pieces such as this Popsicle table were a natural fit for the Knoll portfolio. As well as commissioning new pieces from up-and-coming designers, Knoll had been acquiring the rights to produce work by the likes of Breuer and Mies van der Rohe from the late 1940s on, helping to build awareness of the work of the Bauhaus in the United States and influencing a new generation of designers.

SERIES 7 CHAIR

PLYWOOD

ARNE JACOBSEN
FRITZ HANSEN, 1955

Following on from Charles and Ray Eames's endeavours
with plywood, Arne Jacobsen also recognized the material's
potential to be strong but sculptural. Jacobsen had been
working with Fritz Hansen since 1934, but it was the 1952
'Ant' chair that first captured wider attention. The shape of the
plywood seat and back gave the chair its name and, combined
with its three steel legs, its surprising appearance. Wanting
to create 'a little, light and inexpensive chair', Jacobsen
experimented further, with the Series 7 chair as the result.
Here, the plywood is shaped into the smooth curves of
an hourglass – sensual but simple, and even stackable.

The Series 7 chair became one of the mid-century's bestselling
designs. It's often cited as the chair Christine Keeler posed
on nude during Britain's Profumo Scandal of the 1960s, but in
fact that was just one of many imitations made during the sixty
years since its first release.

MODEL 539 TABLE LAMP

ENAMELLED ALUMINIUM, VINYL AND PLASTIC

GINO SARFATTI
ARTELUCE, *c.* 1955

―――

Gino Sarfatti held a unique position in Italian lighting design.
He was as immersed in the production methods as in the
design and he applied his knowledge to create interesting,
ever-evolving solutions to lighting needs. His systematic
approach is demonstrated in the naming of his designs: Models
numbered 1000 on were chandeliers, while models – such as
this one – numbered 500 on were table lamps.

Sarfatti continued to innovate throughout his hundreds of
designs. Becoming increasingly simplified in form, the lamps
were intended to be adjustable and provide an efficient supply
of light for their users. Thanks to his technical expertise,
combined with design flair, the Arteluce store in Milan, which
opened in 1951, became a focal point for Italian designers
and architects.

VASES

GLASS

VICKE LINDSTRAND
KOSTA, 1955

———

The creative reputation of Victor Emanuel Lindstrand – known as Vicke – is closely tied up with the company Kosta. He was their creative director for over twenty years up to the early 1970s, at the helm in a period when Scandinavian glassware was admired and watched internationally, with Lindstrand's designs taking a starring role.

Although Vicke's background was in commercial art and graphics, it was his work developing new production techniques at Orrefors that helped establish his name. His experimentation continued through the 1950s, creating glassware in deep, rich colours and in naturally inspired shapes that were complemented with abstract patterns. The overall effect was beautiful and deliberately sensual.

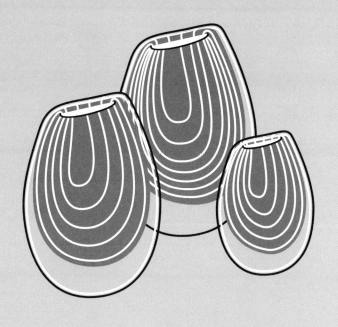

MODEL 5569 COCONUT CHAIR

STEEL AND ALUMINIUM FRAME AND UPHOLSTERED SEATS

GEORGE NELSON
KNOLL, 1955

——

Partly inspired by abstract art by the likes of Alexander Calder, it's the resemblance to a slice of coconut that gives the Model 5569 its more common name. However, George Nelson playfully took this suggestion one step further. He reversed the colours so that it's the outer shell of the chair that is white, and the upholstered 'inside' cushion that's coloured.

Rather than being a formal design intended to make its user sit up straight, the Coconut allowed room to lounge. With its intention of providing comfort, it not only assumed a more relaxed way of sitting but also one of living, perhaps explaining why the design remains so popular today.

MODEL 5670 MARSHMALLOW SOFA

ENAMELLED AND CHROME-PLATED
STEEL FRAMEWORK WITH UPHOLSTERY
PADS COATED IN NAUGAHYDE

GEORGE NELSON
HERMAN MILLER, 1956

———

George Nelson's Marshmallow sofa is as playful as one of his
clocks. A statement piece even now, it would have really stood
out in the mid-1950s, and the Herman Miller catalogue took
pains to reassure potential customers that, 'despite its
astonishing appearance, this piece is very comfortable'. Its
eighteen cushions made it colourful too and the sofa looks
like a Pop piece ahead of its time. However the design was
actually discontinued in the 1960s. It had to be handmade and
was so expensive to produce that, at the time, it was only ever
released in limited numbers.

This sofa is one of the designs attributed to Nelson that is likely
to have been the work of someone else in his studio – Irving
Harper, in this case, who also contributed to the design
of the equally forward-looking Ball clock.

NEST OF TABLES

ELM AND BEECH

LUCIAN ERCOLANI
ERCOL, 1956

———

Ercol are among the few post-war British furniture manufacturers that still exist today and these nesting tables remain one of their most popular designs. Founded by Lucian Ercolani in 1920, the company succeeded in industrializing what previously had been craft processes. By the height of their fame in the 1950s, Ercol were renowned for combining traditional British forms with a Scandinavian sensibility, and all for an attainable price.

While these tables are highly practical – nesting tables were perfect for smaller spaces – they also reflect the more organic look that made Ercol's designs so appealing, with the rounded 'pebble' tops showcasing the natural grain of the wood. Simple, stylish and well made, they are distinctly Ercol.

MODELS 670 AND 671

ROSEWOOD PLYWOOD, ENAMELLED ALUMINIUM AND LEATHER UPHOLSTERY

CHARLES AND RAY EAMES
HERMAN MILLER, 1956

———

It's said the Eameses' friend, the film director Billy Wilder, was the inspiration behind this lounger, and that it was created to fulfil his desire for a modern, comfortable chair. Wilder certainly owned an early prototype, as well as posing in the chair for a 1980s advertising campaign.

But, like the RAR rocking chair, this is another example of the Eameses reinventing traditional furniture for modern living. The model 670 was a new version of the English club chair, designed for relaxing into. Plywood is combined with leather upholstery to create a look that's been described as being as warm and receptive as a baseball mitt.

With this in mind, an expanded version of the chair was more recently released – able to support the increased size of 21st-century bodies in the complete comfort the Eameses (and Billy Wilder) would have expected.

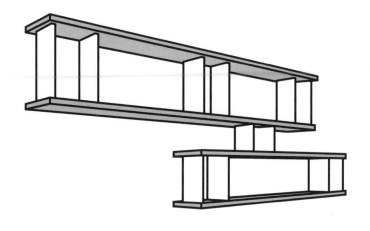

NUAGE BIBLIOTHÈQUE

ASH, ENAMELLED STEEL AND ALUMINIUM

CHARLOTTE PERRIAND
ATELIERS JEAN PROUVÉ FOR GALERIE STEPH SIMON, c. 1956

———

Through her work with Le Corbusier and his cousin Pierre Jeanneret, Charlotte Perriand was behind some of the most famous 'machine age' designs of the interwar period, including the LC4/B306 chaise longue. While this aesthetic continued to influence her approach to design, an extended period in Japan and Vietnam in the 1940s also had an impact, notably by increasing the use of natural materials in her work.

It's thought that the Nuage bookcase was initially designed while Perriand was in Japan although it wasn't realized until much later. It was a modular design, including shelves, units and sliding doors – perhaps inspired by the traditional architecture of Japan – that could be adjusted according to its user's needs and taste, making it the perfect accessory to Perriand's belief in the 'art of living'. Cassina's recent reissue proves how this pioneering design continues to excel in the art of adaptability.

MODEL 150 TULIP CHAIR

LACQUERED FIBREGLASS AND ENAMELLED CAST ALUMINIUM WITH A VINYL-COATED CUSHION

EERO SAARINEN
KNOLL, 1956

The Tulip chair, along with the rest of the Pedestal range (as it was officially called), sprang from Eero Saarinen's desire to liberate the world's interiors from what he described as 'the slum of legs'. His solution was to replace multiple chair and table legs with one simple stem.

Rigorous testing went into this effortless-looking chair, including prototypes trialled on friends and family at Saarinen's home. One article revealed how the chair arms were subjected to a 300-pound pressure hundreds of times in order to stimulate the effect of a heavy man getting up.

Despite appearances this chair is actually made of two different materials. The shell is moulded fibreglass, while the base is sturdier aluminium given a plastic finish. The entire chair is then presented in one unifying colour – in 1956 a choice of grey, beige, black or, most famously, white.

DINING TABLE

STEEL AND GLASS

PHILIPPE HIQUILY
EDITION GALERIE LACLOCHE, 1956

Philippe Hiquily was primarily a sculptor but his experiments with furniture produced dramatic, sometimes surreal, always unique and highly collectable pieces.

As with his art, Hiquily's furniture was typified by its use of metal. However, rather than the machine-made structures of modernism, these were grand pieces of sculpture in their own right. Sometimes the metal was hammered into the seat of a chair; sometimes it was manipulated into abstract forms, as seen on the legs on this table. Other designs were more disturbing: a giant ant forming the base of one table, for example, or the splayed form of Leda, visible through a glass table top. They were all examples of the sometimes complex interplay between art and design in the mid-century period.

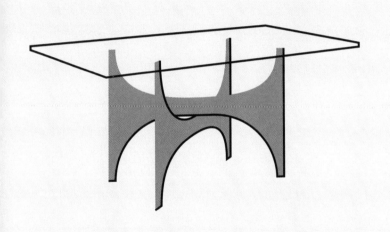

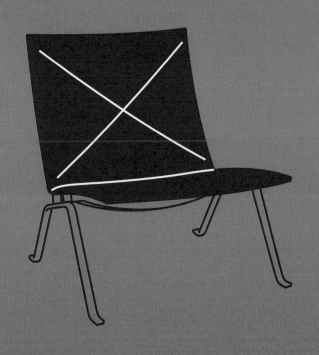

PK22 LOUNGE CHAIR

MATT CHROME-PLATED STEEL AND LEATHER

POUL KJÆRHOLM
E. KOLD CHRISTENSEN, 1956

————

Like that of his fellow Dane Hans Wegner, the work of Poul
Kjærholm is known for imbuing modernist shapes with warmth
and craftsmanship. Unlike Wegner, however, Kjærholm chose to
embrace the materials of the pre-war modern movement, saying
that he considered steel to be 'a material with the same
artistic merit as wood and leather'.

His furniture may look like a feat of artistry but it is the result
of rigorous experimentation. Elegant steel frames were
transformed with the addition of wood, marble and cane as well
as – in the case of the PK22 lounge chair – leather. The chair
is mass-produced furniture, made using the fewest number of
components possible, but it still pulls off the feat of remaining
warm and relatable – so successfully, in fact, that this chair
is still in production today.

WALL CLOCK

ALUMINIUM CASE

MAX BILL
JUNGHANS, 1957

———

Although trained as a silversmith, Max Bill worked as an architect and artist, as well as being a graphic, product and industrial designer. Consistent through his work was – to use the title of a talk he gave – a belief in 'beauty from function and as function'.

Bill had spent two years at the Bauhaus and, post-war, co-founded the short-lived but influential Hochschule für Gestaltung, which was frequently portrayed as its successor. One of the school's achievements was its relationship with the likes of Braun and Junghans, establishing connections that would continue to influence product design in Europe. Bill started working for Junghans himself in 1956, first designing a wall clock and later developing a series of wristwatches. These timepieces could perhaps serve as an ideal reflection of his ideas: ordered, precise and pure.

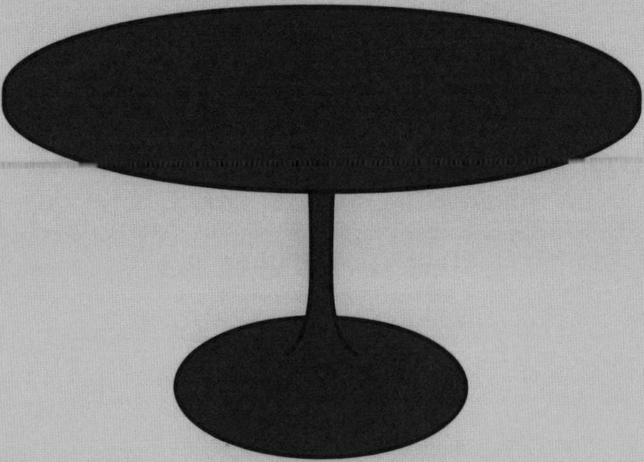

TULIP DINING TABLE

ENAMELLED ALUMINIUM

EERO SAARINEN
KNOLL, 1957

––––

In 1957, *Design* magazine introduced its readers to
Eero Saarinen's Pedestal range of tables and chairs –
more commonly known as the Tulip – describing them as
'a revolutionary concept in furniture design'. Almost sixty
years on, they still look revolutionary, ready for a future
we've yet to reach.

Saarinen applied his architect's eye to his furniture, carefully
considering when and where to place his designs and how they
should look with someone sitting on or at them. He described
such decisions as a 'sculptor's choice', and the resulting Tulip
chairs and tables are undeniably sculptural, endowing modern
materials with a stately dignity. This was the Space Age at
its most stylish.

CANDELABRA

WROUGHT IRON AND GLASS

ERIK HÖGLUND
KOSTA BODA, 1957

———

It was in the 1950s that Scandinavia would receive international attention for its innovative glassware. This was, in part, thanks to the major companies using freelance designers. As they were often also employed in other fields of design, this ensured their work remained forward-thinking and in tune with contemporary interiors and tastes.

Höglund was one such designer. A former student of Stockholm's University College of Art, Craft and Design, he was especially known for the designs he produced for Kosta Boda – a company formed by the merging of two Swedish glassworks – for over two decades from 1953. Here, Höglund has given the traditional form of the candelabra a modernist makeover, with circular glass pendants used to add drama to a pared-back wrought iron framework.

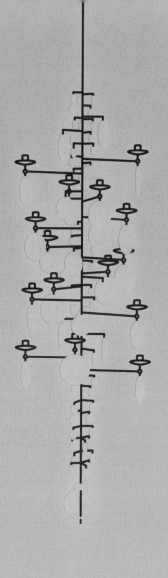

CHERNER ARMCHAIR

WALNUT PLYWOOD

NORMAN CHERNER
PLYCRAFT, 1958

———

Like many other post-war designs, the Cherner chair
explores the possibilities of plywood. Here the material is
at its most sculptural, with elegant ribbons forming arms
and the distinctive outline that has made it one of the most
famous mid-century chairs.

The chair cemented its status as an icon of American design
when the painter Norman Rockwell was pictured in one on the
cover of the *Saturday Evening Post* in 1961. For that reason
it's also sometimes known as the Rockwell Chair.

Although best known for plywood furniture, Norman Cherner's
work also encompassed glass, lighting and pre-fabricated
housing. He shared his theories through books with appealing-
sounding titles such as *Make your own Modern Furniture* and
How to Build a House for Less than $6,000.

ARTICHOKE LAMP

ENAMELLED ALUMINIUM AND STEEL

POUL HENNINGSEN
LOUIS POULSEN, 1958

———

The Artichoke is the Modernist's chandelier, its 72-leaf layered petals making it one of the most commonly recognized pieces of mid-century design. Although Poulsen created more than 100 designs for lamps over his lifetime, this remains the best known – a stylish encapsulation of his desire to achieve 'harmony in lighting'. It was the result of systematic experimentation – adjusting the size and shape of the shade, exploring different materials and colours – with the aim of disguising and softening the glare of electric bulbs. The Artichoke can claim to provide '100% glare-free light' in addition to offering striking, sculptural design.

The Artichoke was commissioned for the Langelinie Pavillonen restaurant in Copenhagen, where it still hangs. It also remains in production, continually sought after, with much of the production process still done by hand. Such is the collector's market, there was even a limited edition gold leaf version produced in 2010.

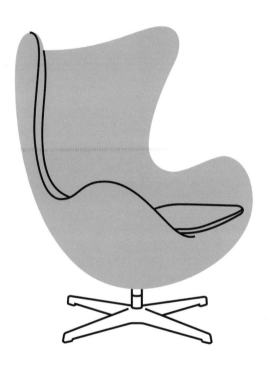

EGG CHAIR

LEATHER AND PLASTIC WITH AN ALUMINIUM BASE

ARNE JACOBSEN
FRITZ HANSEN, 1958

———

No detail was too small to be overlooked by Arne Jacobsen's design philosophy. This was seen to its fullest extent in the SAS Royal Hotel in Copenhagen, where Jacobsen was responsible for everything from the teaspoons to the building itself. This commission also produced some of his most famous pieces, including the Swan and Egg chairs, and the AJ Lamp. Today, just one room of the hotel – number 606 – remains faithful to Jacobsen's original design.

The Egg chair's impact comes from its distinctive graphic outline, with its curved shape creating the impression of sculpture rather than furniture. Still manufactured by Fritz Hansen in a range of fabric and leather upholstery, the chair can also be bought with a matching footstool, making it perfect for relaxing in mid-century style.

PH 5 PENDANT LAMP

ENAMELLED ALUMINIUM AND STEEL

POUL HENNINGSEN
LOUIS POULSEN, 1958

——

Poul was primarily a journalist and writer, but his interest in lighting meant that he designed over a hundred lamps during his lifetime. Each lamp was an investigation into realizing his aim of echoing the soft effects of candlelight with electric lighting.

Henningsen's long-standing relationship with Louis Poulsen began in 1924 and his very first lamp won a prize the following year, at the famous exhibition of decorative arts. The PH 5 was Henningsen's first lamp designed to work with any kind of light source, including even Christmas lights! True to his intention, the PH 5, which remains in production, has been kept updated as new lighting sources have been developed, including a modified design for energy-saving bulbs that was introduced in 1994.

DAF CHAIR

FIBREGLASS, CHROME-PLATED STEEL AND ALUMINIUM

GEORGE NELSON & ASSOCIATES
HERMAN MILLER, 1958

In 1961, George Nelson was pictured in *Playboy* with the likes of Charles Eames, Eero Saarinen and Harry Bertoia, alongside the headline 'Designs for Living'. 'Unfettered by dogma', the copy read, 'the creators of contemporary American furniture have a flair for combining functionalism with aesthetic enjoyment.' The DAF chair ('Desk Armchair Fixed') shows how Nelson's design was part of the American aesthetic, with the use of fibreglass reflecting the innovations of Charles and Ray Eames, and the sweeping forms of its shell suggesting the influence of abstract art.

However, the design is credited to George Nelson '& Associates' and it is believed that Charles Pollock, who worked for Nelson, was largely responsible for it. As was typical for the period, the chair went out under the name of the studio's principal designer.

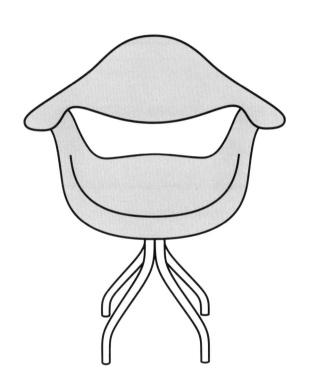

MODEL 2261 SUNFLOWER
WALL CLOCK

LACQUERED PLYWOOD, LAMINATED
ASH PLYWOOD AND BRASS

GEORGE NELSON
HOWARD MILLER CLOCK COMPANY, 1958

——

If Nelson's Ball clock could be interpreted as an abstracted
flower, his Sunflower clock reveals its natural inspiration much
more blatantly, even if it was originally marketed as the less
evocative 'Model 2261'. As with the Ball clock, this design
is made from materials that echo those used in fashionable
furniture designs of the period, in this case, plywood.

It's estimated that George Nelson designed around 150
different clocks for Howard Miller – the son of the furniture
manufacturer Herman Miller – and, in the 1950s, their forms
were inspired by everything from eyes to pretzels. His 'Zoo
Timers', from the 1960s, are clocks shaped as elephants, fishes
and owls, with a selection still available through Vitra.

PANTON CHAIR

INJECTION-MOULDED PLASTIC

VERNER PANTON
VITRA, 1958

———

While the prototype dates back to the late 1950s, it wasn't until 1968 that Vitra perfected the technology necessary to successfully produce Verner Panton's one-piece, plastic 'S'-shaped chair.

While its colour and material echo the carefree spirit of the 1960s, the stackable Panton chair is surprisingly practical. Thanks to being mass-produced, it's also surprisingly affordable.

But it's really the Panton chair's visual appeal – with its almost magical cantilevered form – that helped make it such an instant success and accounts for its continued popularity today. Among many high-profile appearances, it has graced the cover of *Vogue* alongside Kate Moss and, in 1970, was used as a prop in a provocative *Nova* magazine feature called 'How to Undress in Front of Your Husband'.

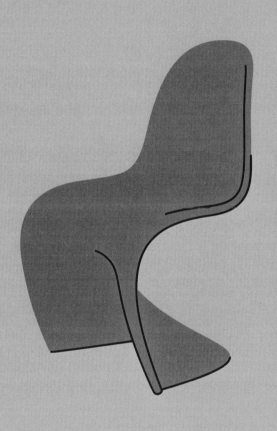

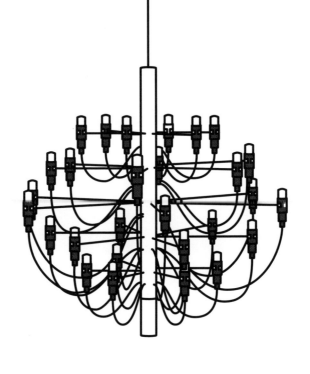

MODEL 2097 CHANDELIER

BRASS

GINO SARFATTI
ARTELUCE, 1958

Gino Sarfatti's designs were known for stripping lighting design down to its essential elements. As the Model 2097 chandelier demonstrates, that was no barrier to creating beauty.

The Model 2097 wasn't an ornate design: brass or chrome-plated arms radiated from a central tube to hold a total of either 30 or 50 bare bulbs. However, the flexes for the bulbs are as much a design feature as the brass fixture – gently draped, they recall the curved arms of traditional chandeliers. Witty and elegant in its apparent simplicity, the Model 2097 remains in production today, albeit with Flos, the company to which Sarfatti sold Arteluce in 1973.

MORRIS MINI MINOR

ALEC ISSIGONIS
IITTALA, 1959

——

The Morris Mini Minor, ultimately known as the Mini, was
the British Motor Corporation's attempt to address the trend
for more compact cars, as illustrated by the success of the
VW Beetle and the Fiat 500. Greek-born, British-educated
designer Alec Issigonis broke new ground with his design for the
Mini, which included front-wheel drive and a transverse engine
that freed up space for three passengers and even a small boot.
Crucially, at three metres long, the Mini came in at the same
size as the Fiat 500.

Over the years, and through subsequent variations, the Mini's
distinctly British design has continued to inspire affection,
whether seen on the roads of Turin in *The Italian Job* or on
the streets of Swinging London – so much so it inspired Mary
Quant to name her equally compact mini skirt in its honour.

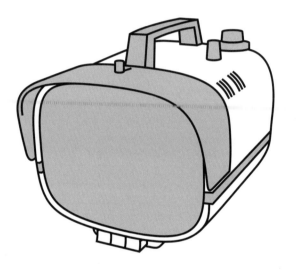

8 301 W PORTABLE TELEVISION

SONY CORPORATION, 1959

––––

Founded in Japan in 1946 by Masaru Ibuka and Akio Morita, Sony wanted to 'always do what has never been done before'. They initially applied that principle to developing radios and tape recorders before turning their attention to the growing consumer market for televisions.

Part of the reason behind their success was their quick uptake of new technologies. Sony introduced the first Japanese transistor radio in 1955 and the 8 301 was the first mass-market portable TV (supplied with its own carrying case). Sony, who also established a reputation for their style, deliberately made this model look different from home televisions, giving it rounded edges and a design based on maximizing the screen area. The 8 301 broke new ground and helped fuel the growing appetite for personal electronics, an area that Sony would tap into so successfully with their later Walkman.

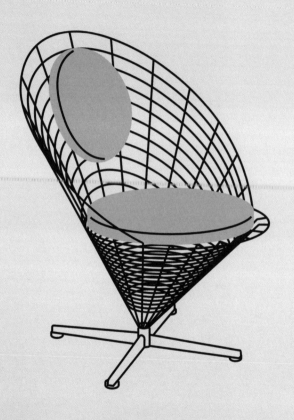

MODEL K2 WIRE CONE CHAIR

CHROME-PLATED STEEL WITH AN
UPHOLSTERED PAD SEAT

VERNER PANTON
PLUS-LINJE, 1959

———

The success of Verner Panton's Wire cone chair illustrates
the appetite for new and innovative design that prevailed in
the 1950s. His upholstered cone chair, originally designed
for a restaurant, had captured the imagination of a worldwide
audience when it was released commercially. According to
Panton, the police ordered the chair to be removed from
a New York shop window, as so many people had gathered
to look at it.

This wire version replicates that startling sculptural form, but
using a perhaps even more surprising material. Panton saw his
design's universal appeal from the off, even suggesting a cone
chair for children. It wasn't until 2003 that this scaled-down
version was actually put into production.

606 UNIVERSAL SHELVING

POWDER-COATED STEEL

DIETER RAMS
VITSŒ, 1960

Dieter Rams' 606 Universal Shelving is an extension of the principles behind his Braun audio systems, with the elements able to stand alone or be components of a larger system. Indeed, Rams specifically designed his Audio 1 system to be displayed on its shelves. His aim was to create a flexible shelving and storage system made from a limited number of components.

In a 1976 speech Rams explained that 'a product must be functional in itself but also must function as part of a wider system: the home'. Deliberately unassuming, the shelving would – he claimed – work alongside furniture from any era or by any designer. It can be easily expanded or taken apart, depending on need. It is a product for life.

Its sales seem to confirm his argument. The shelving has been in continuous production since 1960. Vitsœ also proudly claim that over half their orders come from existing customers.

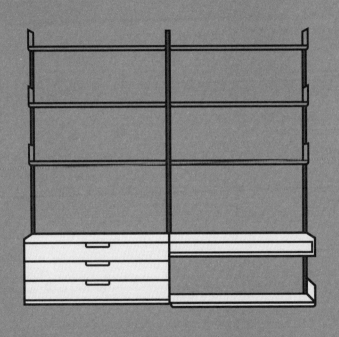

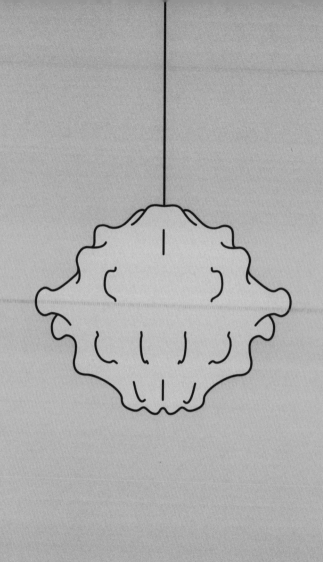

TARAXACUM PENDANT LIGHT

SPRAYED FIBREGLASS OVER A METAL FRAME

ACHILLE CASTIGLIONI &
PIER GIACOMO CASTIGLIONI
FLOS, 1960

The Castiglioni brothers elevated lighting from a functional object
to a desirable consumer item in its own right. Their playful and
innovative designs explored the use of ready-made elements
as well as, as in the case of the Taraxacum lights, the latest
technology. The lights are made from a metal frame sprayed
with liquid polymer which, when solid, forms a strong, flexible
membrane. Their soft, almost organic forms belie their inspiration
– it's said the brothers first saw the polymer being used to protect
American military tanks against bad weather.

A vital part of the Italian post-war design scene, the Castiglioni
brothers helped raise the status of industrial design (both were
founder members of the ASI, *Associazione per il Disegno
Industriale*), and boosted Italy's reputation for excellence in
lighting. Their designs were a sign of the post-war 'Italian
economic miracle' as much as Vespas and coffee machines.

MODEL AT 304 DROP-LEAF DINING TABLE

TEAK AND BRASS

HANS WEGNER
ANDREAS TUCK, c. 1960

By 1960, Hans Wegner was well known internationally for his designs, particularly his Sawbuck and Wishbone chairs of the 1950s and the slightly earlier 501, often referred to simply as 'the chair'. But while many of his contemporaries had relocated to make the most of the opportunities offered in the United States, Wegner chose to remain in Denmark, continuing his work with Danish manufacturers – in this case Andreas Tuck.

This table shows the attention to detail that was a signature of Wegner's style, with the gentle curves of its legs providing the focal point. The functional brass mechanism is seamlessly merged into the overall effect of the design, underlining another reason why Wegner's designs are so loved. Despite their obvious artistry, they are also very practical.

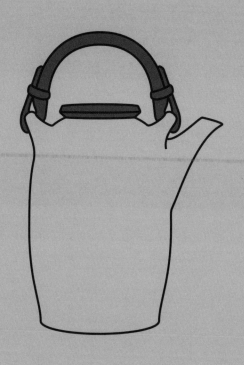

TEAPOT

GLAZED STONEWARE WITH
BAMBOO HANDLE

LUCIE RIE
c. 1960

——

Lucie Rie's work offers an alternative voice in the story of mid-century ceramics, especially when seen alongside the designs of Hans Coper, with whom she shared a studio for over ten years from 1948. Both arrived in London as émigrés and, post-war, established a reputation for themselves as ceramic artists whose work engaged as much with ancient traditions of ceramics as with modern design.

Rie limited herself to working with a small number of ceramic shapes, experimenting again and again to study the effects of different textures and glazes, as seen on this teapot. The results often deliberately evoke a history – a contrast to other designs of the period that revelled in their newness – but, like the folk traditions drawn on by Scandinavian ceramicists, looked equally at home in a mid-century room.

COFFEE TABLE

WALNUT

GEORGE NAKASHIMA
WIDDICOMB, 1961

———

Combining the traditions of his Japanese–American heritage, George Nakashima created pieces that celebrated craftsmanship and uniqueness, rather than conforming to the era's taste for mass production.

Nakashima would describe himself as a woodworker rather than a designer. His pieces highlight the inherent merits of the materials he used, whether spotlighting the characteristics of a slab of walnut as used in this coffee table, or allowing the natural outline of a piece of wood to determine the final shape of the furniture. His pieces were often made for commissions; this table is a rare example of a design he gave to a company for commercial production.

TACCIA LAMP

GLASS, ENAMELLED ALUMINIUM AND STEEL

ACHILLE CASTIGLIONI &
PIER GIACOMO CASTIGLIONI
FLOS, 1962

———

In contrast to the organic shapes of their Taraxacum lights, the Castiglioni brothers' Taccia lamp appeared to be based on strictly geometric forms. However, that made it no less eye-catching. The Taccia consisted of a glass hemisphere that appeared to balance on top of a fluted enamelled aluminium cylinder base.

Although undeniably elegant, the design was led by function rather than form alone. Like the Arco floor lamp, which was designed in the same year and remains the Castiglioni brothers' most famous creation, this lamp is stripped of unnecessary elements. Instead, attention was focused on the lighting effects created by the lamp and how that might work for its owner. Here, the glass sphere diffuser could simply be adjusted to direct the light according to need.

STUDEBAKER AVANTI

RAYMOND LOEWY
STUDEBAKER CORPORATION, 1962

———

Raymond Loewy's prolific output can be explained through his MAYA principle. Standing for 'Most Advanced Yet Acceptable', it underlined the value he placed on pushing on design, but equally the importance of not losing customers in the process. The Avanti certainly felt ahead of its time – with a more European look, it was intended to appeal to younger customers – as emphasized by its name, which means 'forward' in Italian.

It was a sleek design – intended to have no straight lines at all – omitting the chrome detailing that was common on American cars of the period. Loewy pioneered such streamlining not only because of the way it looked, but also because he believed it would make cars faster and more efficient. He would also be responsible for introducing this feature of vehicle design into the home, with his designs that encompassed everything from streamlined fridges to the curves of Coca-Cola bottles.

POLYPROP CHAIR

INJECTION-MOULDED POLYPROPYLENE PLASTIC WITH LIGHTWEIGHT TUBULAR STEEL LEGS

ROBIN DAY
S. HILLE & CO., 1963

––––

Unlike some mid-century classics, the polyprop chair isn't the stuff of high-end galleries. It can be readily found in schools, hospitals, even stadiums, across the world. The chair's ubiquity shows how successfully Robin Day achieved his aim of producing a design that was affordable, durable and fit for purpose. Day saw how injection-moulding polypropylene, which had recently been introduced to the UK, could enable the mass production of a lightweight, all-in-one seat. This shell could then be combined with different legs and bases. Once only available in grey, flame and charcoal shades, polyprop chairs came to be produced in a rainbow of colours perfect for the explosion of Pop that was to follow.

Although they rarely collaborated, Robin Day and his wife, the textile designer Lucienne, were often compared to Charles and Ray Eames. Together, the couple injected some glamour into the British design scene, even appearing in a vodka advert together.

LETTERA 32 PORTABLE TYPEWRITER

MARCELLO NIZZOLI
OLIVETTI, 1963

———

Sleek, streamlined, desirable – it's thanks to the Italian company Olivetti that products such as typewriters could be described in these terms. The Lettera 32 is an update of the Lettera 22, the most influential typewriter of the 1950s, and both are portable and practical, but undeniably good-looking. Marcello Nizzoli's design meant that the streamlining seen on modern cars and trains also found a place in the home and office.

Adriano Olivetti, the visionary head of the company, declared that 'there is nothing in me but the future' and his forward thinking encompassed everything from staff welfare to sophisticated marketing campaigns. Olivetti were honoured with an exhibition at New York's Museum of Modern Art in 1952, confirming their allure. But, despite appearances, the days of the typewriter were numbered. The year after the release of the Lettera 32, Olivetti would launch the Programma 102, the world's first personal computer.

PENGUIN DONKEY MARK 2 BOOKCASE

PLYWOOD WITH LEGS IN CHERRY WOOD

ERNEST RACE
ISOKON, 1963

———

The Penguin Donkey had originally been conceived in 1939, designed by Egon Riss specifically – as the name might suggest – to hold Penguin paperbacks, but production was halted by the war. When Jack Pritchard briefly revived his Isokon business in the 1960s, he asked Ernest Race to revisit the design.

The reasons were mainly practical, as the original Isokon pieces needed to be altered to allow for changes in how plywood was manufactured. Race's version was much simpler – available for self-assembly – and much straighter. A flat top replaced the Donkey's previous curves, meaning it could now be used as a side table. It wasn't the only Riss design revisited by Race: he also gave the Bottleship – a combined bookcase, cocktail cabinet and magazine rack – a similar makeover.

In the 21st century, the Penguin Donkey would be reinterpreted once again, this time courtesy of Shin and Tomoko Azumi.

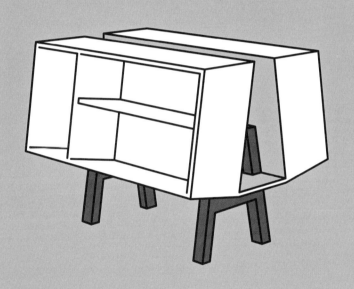

CORONA CHAIR

CHROME-PLATED STEEL AND VINYL

POUL VOLTHER
ERIK JØRGENSEN, 1964

———

The Corona chair is one of the most distinctive and popular examples of mid-century design, with yearly sales now at almost 3,000. Celebrated for its shape and the ellipse-like pattern of its seating pads, the chair demonstrates Danish craftsmanship reinvented for the Space Age.

For a long time, however, the chair was much less well known. It was originally designed in 1961 in wood, with the use of individual cushions supposedly devised as a response to post-war shortages of material. That was followed by this steel-framed version in 1964 but its general success didn't come until a third version was launched in 1997. Poul Volther had by then enjoyed a long career, both as a designer and teacher. It was only thanks to the persistence and devotion of his manufacturer, Erik Jørgensen, that Volther finally saw his design celebrated as the classic it clearly always was.

TS 502 PORTABLE RADIO

RICHARD SAPPER AND MARCO ZANUSO
BRIONVEGA, 1964/2010

———

Richard Sapper studied economics and engineering
in Germany, while Marco Zanuso studied architecture
in Italy. Their collaboration would not only impact the
Italian manufacturing industry, but would also change how
consumers worldwide expected their phones, TVs and
radios to look.

Together, the duo embraced new technologies that meant such
products could now be portable. This TS 502 radio was made
into a desirable product, available in colours as Pop as the music
it could broadcast.

The design rethought the potential form of a radio, with its
publicity claiming that, 'open or closed this radio is an elegant
unit'. It opened into two cubes – one housing the speaker and
the other the receiver – with grooves in the hinges to carry the
necessary cables between the two boxes. Even on its reissue
in 2010, this radio still managed to look like the future.

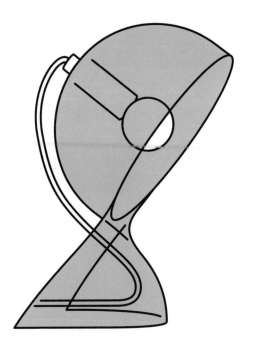

DALÙ TABLE LIGHT

ABS PLASTIC

VICO MAGISTRETTI
ARTEMIDE, 1965

––––

The Dalù illustrates why Vico Magistretti's lighting of the 1960s and '70s is often seen as setting the standard for Space Age style. Its shape chimed with the mood of the time, echoing the helmet hats that appeared on the catwalk from the likes of Pierre Cardin. But despite its futuristic form, the lamp doesn't look alienating.

Magistretti's experiments not only proved that plastic could be aesthetically attractive, but also that it had its own unique properties worthy of exploration. This lamp contains three visible components – the bulb, the flex and the plastic body – but its transformation into a desirable piece of design lies in the appeal of the twists, curves and colour of the plastic element alone.

BALL CHAIR

GEL-COATED FIBREGLASS AND
UPHOLSTERY ON AN ALUMINIUM BASE

EERO AARNIO
ASKO, 1965

————

After early experiments with natural, more traditionally Finnish materials, Aarnio joyfully embraced what he described as the 'total freedom' offered by plastic. The initial prototype for the Ball chair (or Globe chair) was created as a 'big chair' for Aarnio's own home – the chair's height is designed to accommodate his frame – but its Pop colours and futuristic looks chimed perfectly with the mood of the period and it became a commercial success too. Like his later hanging Bubble chair, the cocoon-like interior offers an inviting retreat from the world. Early versions even had their own phone attached to the interior.

The chair's appearance in 1960s TV programmes like *The Prisoner* and films such as *Moon Zero Two* have made it an easy visual shortcut for evoking the Space Age style, resulting in its appearance in everything from countless fashion shoots to *Mars Attacks!*

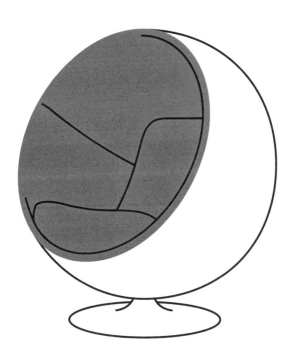

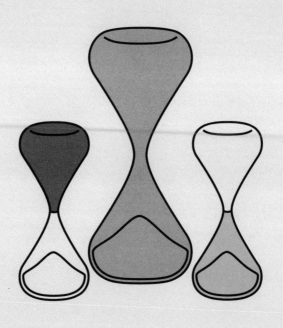

CLESSIDRE SAND TIMER

GLASS

PAOLO VENINI
VENINI & C., *c.* 1965

———

From the late 1940s, through the 1950s and beyond, Venini
& C. were a catalyst for the rebirth of the Italian glass industry.
Based in the traditional glassmaking centre of Murano, they
revived neglected techniques as well as inventing new ones.
Fresh forms and new ideas were introduced by virtue of
working with international artists and designers such as
Tapio Wirkkala and Gio Ponti.

At the heart of the business was its owner, Paolo Venini,
known for closely collaborating with designers – most famously
with Bianconi on the Fazzoletto 'Handkerchief' vase – but also
designing many key pieces himself. His Clessidre sand timers
are one such example – hourglass shapes combining two bold
colours to create an undeniably modern look.

RR126 STEREO

ACHILLE CASTIGLIONI &
PIER GIACOMO CASTIGLIONI
BRIONVEGA, 1965

With lighting such as the Arco floor lamp or the Taccia table lamp, the Castiglioni brothers had created designs that placed their users' needs to the fore. Why should a stereo be any different? As well as providing astonishing Space Age looks, the RR126 was deliberately versatile, with speakers that could either be positioned on its side or the top of the stereo, depending on its owner's preference. As with much Italian design of the period, it married technological advancements with craftsmanship, with the speakers and wood cabinet made by hand.

Brionvega was founded in 1945 and was known for its innovation and high quality. Although it went out of business in the early 1990s, several of its designs have since been reissued by other brands, including the RR126, albeit with the addition of a CD/DVD player to bring its functions into line with the 21st century.

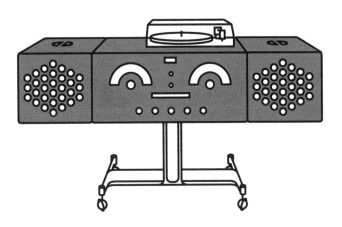

CHILDREN'S WIRE CHAIR

ENAMELLED STEEL

HARRY BERTOIA
KNOLL, c. 1965

―――

Knoll were known for their support of up-and-coming designers, a policy rewarded by the almost immediate success of Harry Bertoia's metal furniture. The range, which also included the famous Diamond chair of 1952, was made from a lattice of steel rods that were shaped to accommodate the contours of the human form. Bertoia considered these designs as he would do a piece of art. As he said, 'If you look at the chairs, they are mainly made of air like sculpture. Space goes right through them.' But, despite their delicate appearance, the chairs are actually extremely strong.

The success of these designs gave Bertoia more freedom to pursue his interest in experimenting with sound and sculpture – art that, once again, was frequently conjured from wire and rods.

TG60 TAPE RECORDER

DIETER RAMS
BRAUN, 1965

As head of Braun's design department for over 30 years, Dieter Rams established a new visual language for the electronic age. Calculator and tape recorder alike were subject to his carefully articulated and rigorously applied principles of good design. Objects should be easy to use, long-lasting and beautiful to look at.

Objects such as the TG60 benefitted from the greater flexibility afforded by new transistor technologies. The TG60 could be laid horizontally or wall-mounted like a work of art. It could be added to and work alongside other units, such as the TS45 and L450 control unit and speaker, without compromising its appearance or usefulness.

Rams' work was hugely influential. His 1954 SK4 gave the record/radio player its once almost standard clear lid (or 'Snow White's coffin', as it was nicknamed). It's hard to imagine the likes of Apple without reference to Braun's clear and consistent identity.

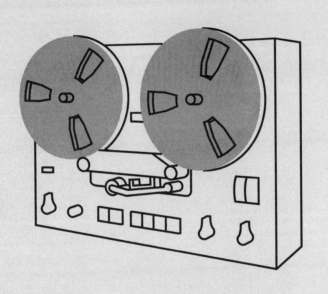

DINING CHAIR

CHROME-PLATED STEEL AND UPHOLSTERY

WARREN PLATNER
KNOLL, c. 1966

———

Warren Platner introduced his chair to cater to the mid-1960s desire for a 'decorative, gentle, graceful kind of design'. He transformed steel into something sensuous, distinctly modern but with an old-fashion elegance.

'Why separate support from the object?' he wondered, and so, ingeniously, created the curving structure of his chairs and their accompanying tables using a fan of light, thin steel rods, bypassing the need for separate support. Platner's training as an architect also fed into the design, as he considered how the chair would look in a space. It would be, he believed, 'complementary to the person sitting in it'.

Platner's designs captured the mood of the time and were an instant success. They've been in production ever since, with the most iconic simply referred to as 'the Platner chair'.

GRILLO PHONE

RICHARD SAPPER AND MARCO ZANUSO
SIEMENS, 1966

———

Sapper and Zanuso's Grillo took the telephone into a whole other realm. Gone were the cradle and the handset – this plastic shell housed dial, ear and mouthpiece in one. When the phone was picked up, the mouthpiece would fall down, also picking up the line. The name comes from the sound of the phone's ring: 'Grillo' means cricket. The sound comes from the plug rather than the phone itself.

While dial phones may have been left in the 20th century, the folding phone would go on to be an influence on the design of mobile phone, something the duo – with their knack for creating portable devices – would surely appreciate.

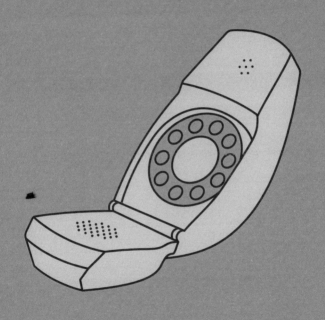

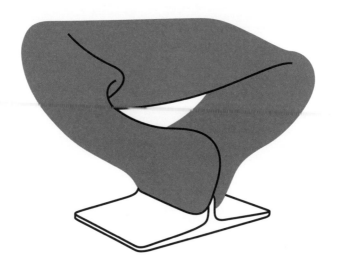

RIBBON ARMCHAIR

LACQUERED WOOD AND UPHOLSTERY

PIERRE PAULIN
ARTIFORT, 1966

When injury frustrated his ambitions to become a sculptor,
Pierre Paulin instead applied his skills to the form of the chair.
His Ribbon design maintains the clean lines of mid-century
modernism, albeit made over in new colours and materials.
But, however eye-catching, his design wasn't based on artistry
alone. He embraced new materials, especially polyurethane
foam, not only because it helped create a more sensuous
shape, but also because it would make his chairs more
comfortable. Design was, in his opinion, 'a mix of invention
and industrial innovation'.

Paulin continued conjuring up ever-inventive forms through
the 1960s. Whether Ribbons, Mushrooms, Tongues or Tulips,
Paulin's bright, bold and beautiful chairs captured the mood
of the decade.

BEOVOX 2500 'CUBE' SPEAKERS

JACOB JENSEN
BANG & OLUFSEN, 1967 TO 1972

———

The Danish brand Bang & Olufsen was founded in the 1920s, but it was during the 1950s that it started working with forward-thinking designers and embracing new technologies to establish the company's reputation for design excellence that continues today. One of those designers was Jacob Jensen.

Jensen was behind some of the company's most distinctive products, such as these unapologetically sculptural and futuristic speakers. Indeed, when New York's Museum of Modern Art held an exhibition devoted to Bang & Olufsen they singled Jensen out for attention. It was only the fifth time the museum had dedicated a display to one firm alone (although Bang & Olufsen's electronic rivals, Braun, had already been honoured), and the objects were praised for their understated elegance, rich materials and 'visual impact on domestic interiors'. They were, as exemplified by these speakers, 'beautiful objects in their own right'.

INSTAMATIC 33

KENNETH GRANGE
KODAK, 1968

——

From trains to razors, pens to kitchen mixers, Kenneth Grange
has shaped the look of many different aspects of British life.
The starting point behind all these designs is, he says, 'the
belief that I can design something better'. That certainly
underpinned his twenty-plus years relationship with Kodak,
which began with a remark – made while working on exhibition
design for the company – on the ugliness of their cameras.

Grange's first design for Kodak was the Box Brownie 44a
in 1959, marketed as a simple camera that anyone could use.
However, it was the Instamatic series, beginning with the
33, that was his and the company's major success. Designed
around the company's easy-load cartridge film, the camera's
appearance was made similarly user-friendly, modern but
accessible. The approach worked, with over 25 million
Instamatics sold worldwide.

VP GLOBE LIGHT

ACRYLIC WITH ENAMELLED AND
CHROME-PLATED STEEL REFLECTORS

VERNER PANTON
LOUIS POULSEN, 1969

Born and educated in Denmark, Verner Panton is
celebrated for his optimistic, futuristic designs that are a
departure from the more naturally inspired forms usually
associated with Danish design. This was particularly evident
in his choice of materials and his favouring of metals and
plastics over wood.

However, Panton's work was informed by some of Denmark's
best known designers. He assisted Arne Jacobsen for two
years and Poul Henningsen was his mentor. There are echoes
of the forms of Henningsen's PH lamps in the Globe light – not
least in that the discs above and below the bulb can be adjusted
to adapt the light to its environment. Secured in its acrylic
sphere, this light is undeniably equipped for the Space Age.

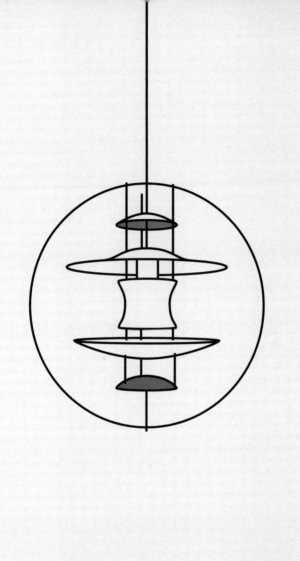

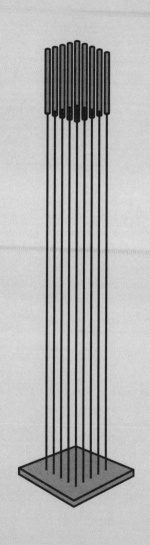

'SONAMBIENT' SCULPTURE

BERYLLIUM, COPPER AND BRASS

HARRY BERTOIA
BERTOIA STUDIO, c. 1970

Bertoia may be best known for his lattice steel furniture, particularly his Diamond chair of 1952, but his oeuvre also encompassed more experimental pieces. The success of designs such as the Diamond gave him the freedom to pursue more creative work. He became particularly renowned for his Sonambient sculptures.

Having been inspired by the sound of one metal wire hitting another, Bertoia made these sculptures by arranging wire rods in different formations. Each grouping varied in form and size and the arrangements were frequently inspired by nature. In addition to making intriguing visual pieces, the sculpture's resulting sounds – described as mysterious and mesmerizing – have been used as the basis for eleven albums.

MODEL 423P OCCASIONAL TABLE

LAMINATED WOOD AND ENAMELLED STEEL

VERNER PANTON
X-DESIGN, *c.* 1971

___

As also demonstrated by his Wire cone chair, Verner Panton's
Model 423P table shows that steel doesn't have to be hard
and industrial – it can also be playful. And, while the cone chair
is based on one simple shape, this table explores two more:
the circle and the cylinder. In addition, it shows how Panton
continued to evolve the language of his designs throughout
his career.

By the early 1970s, Panton was designing complete, futuristic
environments where the shapes and colours of his furniture
were echoed in the textiles, lighting and décor. This table was
part of his Pantonova series, a collection of wire-based furniture
designed and produced for the Varna restaurant in Aarhus,
Denmark. Panton's scheme for the restaurant reflected the
rounded shapes visible in the architecture of the building itself.

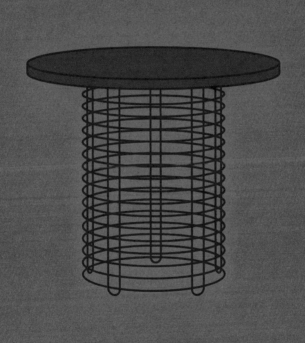

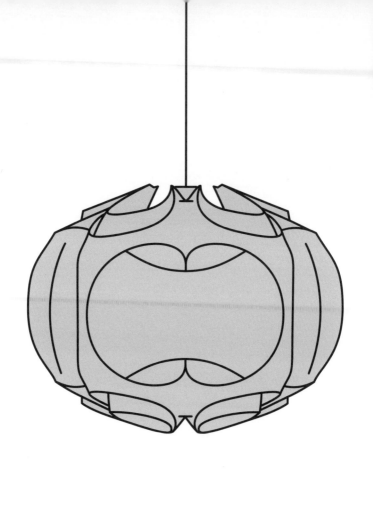

171 PENDANT LAMP

FOLDED PLASTIC

POUL CHRISTIANSEN
LE KLINT, 1971

Like Isamu Noguchi's Akari lights, Le Klint's pendants showed how traditional forms could be reinvented using new materials and new ideas. This family business created and sold hand-made folded paper lampshades and, in the 1950s, moved into plastic shades that echoed the forms of the originals. However, it was the architect and designer Poul Christiansen's designs from the late 1960s to 1987 that really invigorated the company. He replaced what had hitherto been pleats and straight lines with mathematically-inspired curves, as also seen in his famous 172 Sinus lamp.

By day, these were sculptural pieces; by night, when illuminated, they took on an otherworldly dimension. The lamps had practical applications too. The enclosed shape of the base of this lampshade, for example, helps to reduce glare. The 73 pendant variants that are available today remain instantly recognizable as Le Klint, a tradition that still looks contemporary.

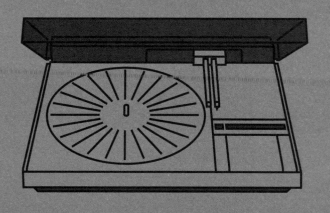

BEOGRAM 4000
RECORD PLAYER

JACOB JENSEN
BANG & OLUFSEN, 1972

———

Danish electronics company Bang & Olufsen remain renowned for the distinctive good looks of their designs, a reputation established in the 1960s and '70s, thanks in part to their relationship with the designer Jacob Jensen.

Mid-century technological advances allowed electronics to be rethought and refined and the Beogram 4000 demonstrates how radically different a record player could look. It was a considered design that could fit alongside other Bang & Olufsen items, sleek and stylish, with even the electronic control pad fully integrated into the design.

The Beogram 4000 pioneered several ideas ahead of larger competitors. The 'tangential tracking' introduced by the second arm meant a record could be played in the same way that it was cut, while a 'danceproof' internal suspension system protected the most sensitive parts of the player from vibrations. This player didn't only look like the future, it sounded like it too.

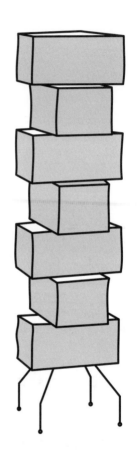

MODEL UF 4-L10 AKARI
FLOOR LAMP

PAPER OVER A STEEL FRAME

ISAMU NOGUCHI
OZEKI AND CO., c. 1975

––––

Beginning with his first lamp in the 1940s, Isamu Noguchi
created new forms for his Akari – meaning 'light' or 'illumination'
– throughout his career. Over the decades, they remained
affordable, accessible pieces of designs. As Noguchi said
himself, 'All you need to start a home are a room, a tatami
and Akari.'

Although simple in form – so simple they have been imitated
many times over – in their naturally inspired, organic shapes
they were representative of Noguchi's idiosyncratic style, which
encompassed furniture and glassware as well as his sculpture
and these lights. 'I do not wish to belong to any school,' he said.
'I am always learning, always discovering.'

ATOLLO TABLE LAMP

ENAMELLED METAL BASE AND REFLECTOR

VICO MAGISTRETTI
OLUCE, 1977

———

Best known for his Space Age lighting designs of the 1960s
and '70s, Vico Magistretti originally trained as an architect and
also worked as a furniture designer.

The Atollo takes the recognizable shape of a table lamp and
reduces it to its elements: a cylinder and a cone topped with
a hemisphere. The choice of finish is equally simple – it came
in either a gleaming white or a sleek black – in keeping with
Magistretti's claim that 'I like concept design, the kind which
is so clear you do not need to draw it.'

Part of Magistretti's success was that his designs married
artistry with usefulness. Despite the reduced nature of its form,
the reflector inside its sphere means that the Atollo emits
a warm and comforting glow.

MODEL NAMES

DESIGNERS

MANUFACTURERS